My Maine

To Mateo & Mikela
Always follow your dreams!
Susan Hersey
2012
(from GG & Tati)

My Maine

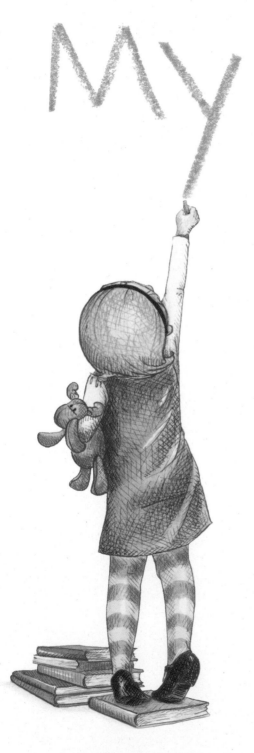

Little Beach Books

By Suzanne Buzby Hersey

Illustrated by Nicole Fazio

Text copyright © Suzanne Buzby Hersey, 2011
Illustrations copyright © Nicole Fazio, 2011

ISBN: 978-0-615-37246-4
Library of Congress Control Number: 2010907240

First Edition

All inquiries should be addressed to:

Little Beach Books
P.O. Box 6148
Falmouth, ME 04105

info@littlebeachbooks.com
www.littlebeachbooks.com
207.878.8804

Printed and manufactured by C&C offset Printing Co. Ltd. in China.
This book was printed on OK Matt Kote Green 100, 100% recycled paper.

Designed by Nicole Fazio Illustration & Design.
The illustrations in this book were executed in watercolor and acrylic ink on Arches paper.
The type is set in Georgia. Cover lettering by Nicole Fazio.

In loving memory of Audie.
Thank you for bringing our family to the beautiful state of Maine.

SBH

My Maine is _____.

Tell us what makes
Maine special!

My Maine is for moose,

county fairs, whoopie pies...

and for shooting stars streaking across summer skies.

My Maine is for wild blueberries
and fresh lobster rolls,

for island escapes
and cool morning strolls.

BAR HARBOR, MAINE

Greetings from Moosehead Lake,

Bar Harbor, Moosehead Lake...

Don't forget L.L. Bean,
for goodness' sake!

Portland is Maine's *largest* city of all.

If you go, I just know
that you'll have a ball!

It has cool museums and souvenir shops,
plus hot chocolate at cafés when the temperature drops.

Augusta is Maine's capital city, you see,

and Maine's state bird is the chickadee.

Listen closely
to hear the birds singing with glee.

Chicka-
dee-dee-
deeee

from the snow-covered tree.

My Maine is known as the Pine Tree State.

Take a deep breath ... doesn't it smell *great*?

From the beautiful lakes
to the mountains so grand,

I guess this is why it's "Vacationland."

The rocky coastline—
nothing beats it!

Kayaking and puffin watches
are guaranteed hits.

Searching for sea glass is fun at low tide,

but don't get discouraged,
as some pieces will hide!

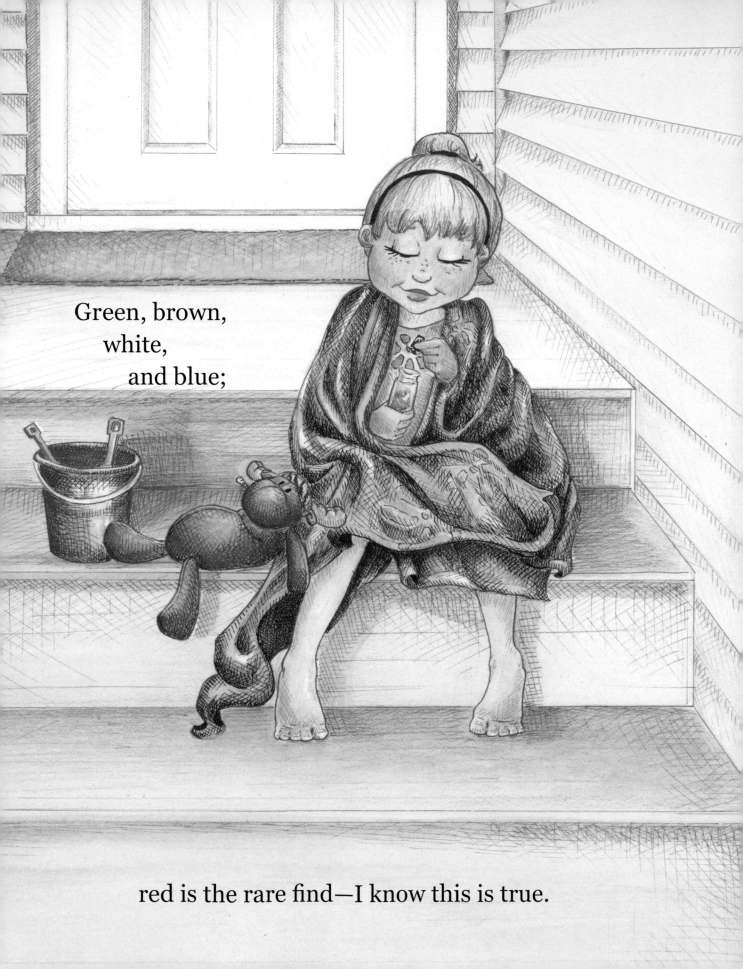

Green, brown,
white,
and blue;

red is the rare find—I know this is true.

Our rainy days are surprisingly fine,

filled with card games,
puzzles,
and family time.

Bright lighthouses guide boats on gray foggy days.

The fog is now lifting—
here come the sun's rays!

Farmers, foresters,
lobstermen, too,

work hard and I'm thankful
for all that they do.

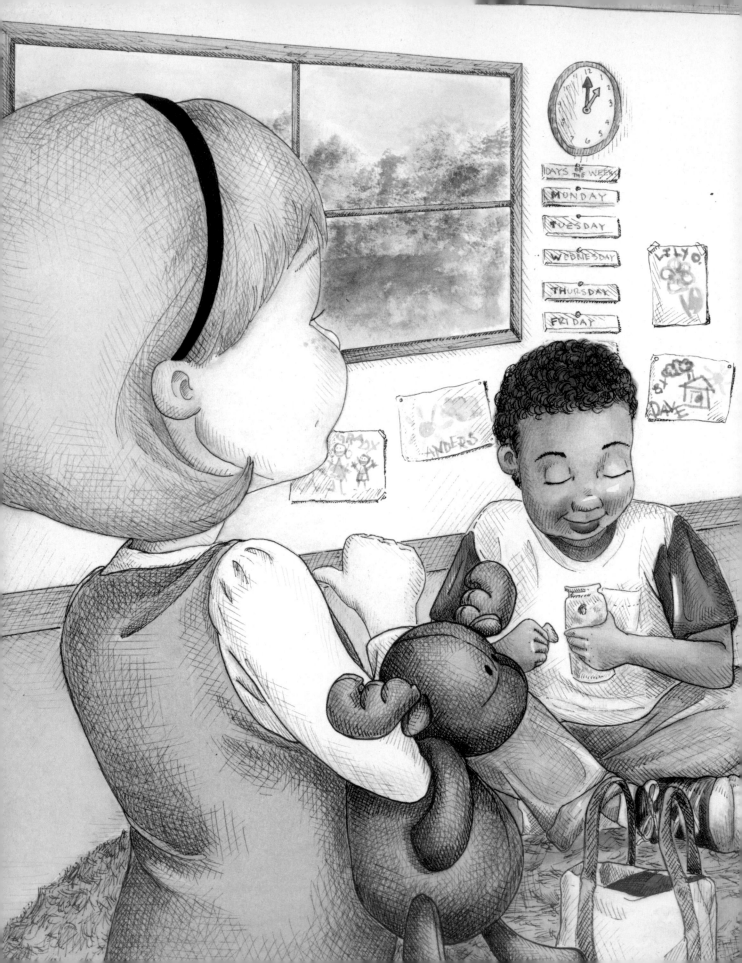

In Maine,
every day is "the way life should be."

It's a "wicked good" life here,
for you and for me!

Suzanne Buzby Hersey

is a firm believer in chasing after your dreams. For as long as she can remember, she has aspired to one day make her home in the state of Maine—and to be an author of children's books. Both of these dreams have now come true. Although she is a native of New Jersey, she grew up spending her summers in Maine's beautiful midcoast region. Upon graduating from the University of New Hampshire, she moved to Maine and began to fulfill her other passion by working with children in a variety of settings. She attributes many of her ideas for creating stories to the children who surround her every day. It was only natural that she chose to create a story that invites readers to share in her love of Maine. Suzanne makes her home in Portland with her husband, Ryan. This is her first children's book.

Nicole Fazio

resides in Portland, Maine, where she works as an illustrator and graphic designer. She graduated with honors from the Hartford Art School in Connecticut. Working primarily with pen and ink and watercolor, Nicole takes great joy in creating beautiful illustrations that will captivate the imaginations of children and be cherished by adults. *My Maine* is Nicole's first children's book.

To see more of Nicole's work, please visit
www.nicolefazioillustration.com